BART STARR

Professional Quarterback

BART

PROFESSIONAL

1973 • New York

STARR

QUARTERBACK

by Tex Maule
illustrated with photographs

FRANKLIN WATTS, INC.

The pictures on the following pages are courtesy of Vernon J. Biever: pp. 5, 20, 23, 28, 31, 35, 38, 41, 43, 44, 50, 53, 56, 59, 67, 68, 73, 77, 78, 81, 83, 84, 86

Library of Congress Cataloging in Publication Data

Maule, Hamilton.
    Bart Starr, professional quarterback.

    1. Starr, Bart.   I. Title.
GV939.S73M3   796.33′2′0924   72-7355
ISBN O-531-02610-8

BART STARR

Professional Quarterback

On a bitterly cold Sunday afternoon in early January, 1968, Bart Starr, quarterback of the Green Bay Packers, took a long step toward being recognized as one of the four or five best quarterbacks in the history of professional football. In his long career, he had scored touchdowns on longer runs and passed for many more, but when he scored from the Dallas Cowboy one-yard line with icy night falling outside the lighted stadium, he underlined his claim to a place in the Professional Football Hall of Fame.

The victory gave the Packers the championship of the National Football League, and they went on to win their second straight Super Bowl game by defeating the Oakland Raiders easily.

But the play that Starr executed on the icy field in Green Bay was the true climax of his great career and the peak moment in the reign of the Green Bay Packers as the finest team in football.

The play came with only eleven seconds left to play in the game and the Packers behind, 17–14. They had used up their last time out, but it was only third down, so an incomplete pass would have stopped the clock and given them an opportunity to tie the game with an almost certain field goal.

Starr had conferred for two minutes with coach Vince Lombardi just before returning to the huddle to call the play, and the two men had made a surprising decision. Probably every one of the frostbitten fans and players in the stadium expected Starr to do the obvious thing—pass. The footing was slippery from the ice that had formed on the field, and on two previous running plays Starr's running backs had been unable to get traction.

Instead, Starr very calmly called a quarterback sneak. He and Lombardi had agreed to gamble on one more running play. "If we can't run it in from the one with all there is at stake in this game, we don't deserve the title," Lombardi had said, and Starr agreed with him.

But it was up to Starr to decide who would carry the ball. Typically, he accepted the responsibility himself, knowing that any back who failed to score on the play would be blamed by the fans and the press for the loss of the game and the championship.

At the snap of the ball, he drove forward behind the broad shoulders and churning legs of Jerry Kramer, his all-pro right guard. Kramer and Ken Bowman, the Green Bay center, wedged big Jethro Pugh, Dallas's defensive tackle, back a precious yard and a half, and Starr dived into the narrow hole, barely getting his chest and arms and the ball over the goal line for the touchdown.

4

The "big play." Starr (15) sprawls over the Dallas goal line with 13 seconds to play in the 1967 NFL championship game. He followed Jerry Kramer's (64) block on Jethro Pugh (75) for the touchdown that won the game for Green Bay.

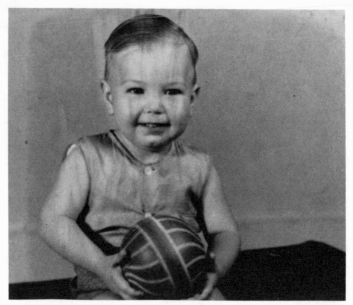

At the age of eighteen months, Bart won second prize in a healthiest baby contest.

Bart at thirteen with his father, a retired Air Force master sergeant.

It was a confident, courageous call, and it took a great quarterback to make the decision and then to make the play work. Starr was and is a great quarterback, but he did not become one easily. The road that led to the Dallas one-yard line and all-pro selection was neither short nor easy.

Bart was born in Montgomery, Alabama, the son of a master sergeant in the United States Air Force who had played football in school. Like most fathers, Sergeant Starr wanted his son to follow in his footsteps, and he gave the young Bart a football almost as soon as he had learned to walk.

"The first football I had was a toy one, just about the size to fit my hand," Bart says. "But I used to spend hours with Dad in the backyard playing catch. I loved football even then, as young as I was, and I have never loved any other sport as well. Even when the going was roughest and it looked like I might not make it in the pros, I enjoyed playing, even practice."

By the time he was twelve, Bart was playing on the equivalent of a Little League team, sponsored by the Montgomery chapter of the Veterans of Foreign Wars.

"I don't remember much about playing on that team," he says. "I remember I was small and I played in the backfield, but I didn't really learn much about how to play the game until I went to junior high school. Football was a big thing in Alabama, and the junior high program was well organized, with good equipment and excellent coaching. Good equipment is important for a youngster because it prevents injury. Good coaching does the same thing, because you learn

7

how to handle yourself and the proper techniques of blocking and tackling. I was lucky to learn early and I was lucky to have a father who always encouraged me. I was a small halfback in junior high, but I played regularly."

At Sidney Lanier High School, his lack of size was a real handicap. The competition was stronger, the players bigger and better, and Bart found himself relegated to the scrub team. He shifted from halfback to quarterback in the tenth grade, but he was the substitute quarterback behind a bigger and older player and he began to grow more and more discouraged.

"Dad did his best to keep my spirits up, but I couldn't see any way I was going to make the first team, and finally one day I decided to quit. I knew how disappointed my dad would be and I had a hard time making myself tell him I was quitting, but when I did, he didn't argue with me."

"Do what you think is best, Son," Sergeant Starr said. "But you can't spend your afternoons lying around and doing nothing. If you don't want to go to practice tomorrow afternoon, I want you to come straight home and I'll have some work for you to do."

"I had to cut down a stand of old corn in the back garden, then clean up the yard and mow the grass," Bart says, laughing. "After a couple of afternoons of that, I finally figured out that football practice was more fun. When I told Dad I had decided to go back to the team, he gave me a little talk on quitting. He waited until I had made up my own mind, but he pointed out that nothing valuable is easy to earn. I had

Starr at the beginning of his senior year at Sidney Lanier High School in Montgomery, Alabama. With him are teammate Bobby Barner and coach Bill Moseley.

more or less figured that out in the back garden chopping down corn, but he helped me to understand it better."

Halfway through the season, the starting quarterback suffered a broken leg and Bart was given a chance. He played well enough to hold the starting job for the next season and a half. During his junior year, the team was undefeated.

"My big play that year was a little like the play against Dallas," Bart said. "We were playing our toughest opponent, and it was late in the game and we were behind. I called a bootleg, swung out wide to my right with the ball on my hip, and when the defense closed in, I hit one of the ends for a touchdown in the end zone. It was an option play; if the defense had dropped off, I could have run the ball in."

His last year at Sidney Lanier, Bart was named to the High School All-America team, and in 1952 he was given a football scholarship at the University of Alabama, where he had always wanted to play.

He earned a varsity letter as a freshman, playing quarterback behind a veteran, but playing well on the few occasions he got into the game. He had learned patience in junior high school and he was not discouraged now.

"I was learning," he says. "It's a big jump from high school to college and I was lucky to play on the varsity as a freshman. That was during the Korean War, and freshmen were eligible to play."

Alabama played Syracuse in the Orange Bowl that season and defeated them easily. Late in the game,

Starr was a punter as well as a passer in high school.

Starr with his two high school coaches just after signing to attend the University of Alabama in 1952. At left, head coach Bill Moseley; right, line coach Matt Lair.

with Alabama well in the lead, Bart went in at quarterback. As usual, he engineered a touchdown, passing to an open receiver. The score gave Alabama a record for the most points ever scored in an Orange Bowl game, although it had nothing to do with the Alabama victory.

By now, Bart had almost reached maturity. He was a little over six feet tall, well built and strong. Even then, he was a serious man, with a thoughtful face dominated by clear, direct blue eyes.

He had, and still has, a faculty for devoting his entire attention to what he is doing. He is a rather quiet man, but he has what in the army is called command presence. In a locker room, on the practice field or in the huddle, he inspires confidence and respect not by loud orders or by harsh criticism but by his own air of self-confidence and knowledge.

Under Bart's guidance the next year, Alabama had another very successful season. Bart, besides playing quarterback well, was the punter and finished second in the nation in punting. Alabama went to the Cotton Bowl to play Rice University at the end of the season, but this time, in spite of all Bart could do, the team lost.

"They beat us pretty bad," Bart says. "We didn't have any excuses, they were just a better team. But I think we were upset by one thing that happened during the game."

This was one of the most unusual incidents in the history of college football. Dicky Moegle, a Rice halfback, was returning an Alabama punt along the sideline in front of the Alabama bench and appeared to have a clear field for a touchdown.

But Tommy Lewis, a young Alabama substitute, became so overwrought that he jumped off the bench, ran on the field, and tackled Moegle. The officials awarded Rice a touchdown, the most severe penalty ever given in a bowl game.

That strange incident and the loss seem, in retrospect, to have been a bad omen for Bart. Early the next season, he hurt his back and missed nearly all of the games, as Alabama slumped.

As so often happens after a team has a bad year, a new coach was brought in for Bart's senior year. Unfortunately for Bart, the new coach believed in the old adage "A new broom sweeps clean."

The new coach decided to rebuild the club by using only his young players, so that, in what should have been his best year as a college player, Bart spent most of his time on the bench and, in the one game he started, he sprained his ankle.

He took his misfortune stoicly, however. He did not relish sitting on the bench, but he bit back his anger and said, when asked what he thought about the new coach and his ideas, "I suppose he is doing what he thinks is best."

It was particularly unlucky that this happened in his senior year, when most college players are very carefully scouted by the professional teams. Since Bart played very little, naturally none of the pro clubs showed much interest in him.

In the annual draft of college seniors, in which the pro club with the worst record for the year drafts first

Starr with Alabama teammates End Curtis Lynch (82), Quarterback Albert Elmore (14), Starr (10), and End Nick Germanos (80), who also played on Bart's team in high school.

In the summer of 1956, Bart's father helped him prepare for his pro tryout with the Green Bay Packers.

and each team, in reverse order of its finish, picks players until twenty per club have been selected, Bart was not chosen until it came time for Green Bay to make its seventeenth choice. He might not have been picked at all had it not been for his friendship with Johnny Dee, the Alabama basketball coach, who knew Jack Vainisi, the Packers' chief scout, very well.

"I might have been picked up later as a free agent," Bart says. "But Johnny talked Vainisi into taking a chance on me. Of course, by the time the clubs get down to the seventeenth round, they're not exactly picking blue-chip players, so it wasn't that much of a chance. But it meant quite a lot to me. I was feeling pretty bad about that time, and I was beginning to lose confidence in myself and even to doubt my ability to play. Oh, I remembered what Dad had said back when I quit in junior high school, but it just seemed like everything was going wrong."

His being drafted ensured that Bart would at least be given the chance to make a pro-football club, and he determined to prepare himself as thoroughly as he knew how. He had learned good habits of hard work and concentration from his father and put these traits to use that summer of 1956.

Bart had married during his junior year at Alabama and he and Cherry, his wife, spent the summer at her parents' home before he reported to the Green Bay training camp. Bart built a frame in the front yard of the house and hung an automobile tire from it by a rope. For hours every day, he practiced throwing a football through the tire from different distances and different angles, sometimes with the tire hanging still, often with it swinging.

"Cherry was my fielder," he says, smiling. "By the end of the summer, she might have made the Packers as a receiver, if she had been big and fast enough. She had the hands."

The hard work paid off when he reported to the Packers in August. There were five candidates for the quarterback job, including Tobin Rote, a veteran who had been the regular quarterback the year before. Bart did not expect to beat Rote out of his job, but he hoped to stick as Rote's substitute at least.

He knew that out of the hundred-odd players in camp, only forty would make the Packer team. The others would be cut from the squad at intervals during the pre-season training, usually after a pre-season game. When a player is cut, he is visited in his room by an assistant coach after dinner and leaves immediately. When cuts are to be made, the players say that the Turk is coming to call. Bart had made up his mind not to be one of the players who meet the Turk.

"I didn't have a sensational training camp my rookie year," Bart said. "Every time the Turk made his rounds, I was afraid I would hear a knock on my door, but somehow I made it. I wasn't sure I had made the team until the final cut, the week before the regular season began. When the Turk passed me by that night, I guess it was one of the happiest moments of my life. I'm still not quite sure why they picked me over some of the others, but I remember I played one good half against the New York Giants in the last couple of weeks, and maybe that was what did it."

Chapter

In his rookie year, Bart roomed with Tobin Rote, the veteran quarterback, and Rote, who had been a starting quarterback for several years, taught him a good deal.

"Tobin was a very tough guy," Bart said. "He had his own style, which wasn't at all like mine, and he was set in it, but he was thoughtful and helpful with me and he gave me some very useful tips. He didn't have to do that, especially since we were competing for the same job, and I really appreciated it."

Even with Rote's help, Starr got in very little playing time during his rookie season, primarily because it almost always takes a college quarterback three or four years to learn the much more complex, difficult offenses and defenses in professional football.

Although he had been a good college passer, he had to learn to throw the ball harder and flatter to beat pro defensive backs. That was one of the many things Rote taught him.

"He watched me throw a few times in practice,

Trainer makes sure Starr's footing will be good against Detroit in 1962.

then stopped me," Bart remembers. " 'Kid, you have got to learn to zip the ball a little more,' he said to me. 'You won't make it in this league throwing cream puffs.' "

All pro players have physical courage or they would not be able to play the game, since it is rough and sometimes dangerous and very few players go through a career without at least one serious injury, while many suffer more than one. Starr, of course, was a courageous man, but Rote, who shrugged off all but the most serious injuries and often played with a sore arm or leg that might have benched another player, set him an example.

"He was rugged," Starr says. "He took some shots that might have put a lot of guys out of action and came right back on the next play and acted as if nothing had happened. He didn't let the punishment affect the way he threw the ball, and that's something else I learned from him. If you start flinching after you've been hit hard a few times, you're through, because everyone in the league will know it and they'll come after you even harder."

The Packers were a long way from a championship team in Bart's first season with them, but he had little to do with their lack of success. The durable Rote played most of the time and, in his brief and infrequent appearances, Starr threw only forty-four passes, about a tenth as many as a starting quarterback like Joe Namath may throw in a season. He completed twenty-four for 325 yards and two touchdowns, showing at least a hint of the kind of quarterback he was to develop into, but he still had a good deal to learn when the 1957 season ended.

The next year Rote left, but Starr was still not the starting quarterback. Somewhat to his dismay, the club acquired Babe Parilli, another veteran, who had been one of Bart's boyhood idols when Parilli had played college football at the University of Kentucky.

"It felt funny, competing with Babe for the job," Bart said. "I guess Scott Hunter, the rookie quarterback we got from Alabama in 1971, must have felt the same way about me."

Starr shared time with Parilli, though, and played longer and more often than he had the year before. With more playing time, he was beginning to learn more about how to read pro defenses so that he could attack them better, but he was not satisfied with his performance. He threw 215 passes and completed 117, but he threw for only three touchdowns.

"That's probably why Babe actually played more than I did," he says. "I really wasn't getting the job done. The only statistic that really counts for a quarterback is how many points you put on the board, and I wasn't putting up many. I still loved football and I enjoyed the life of a professional football player, but I didn't have a very good feeling when I went back to Alabama at the end of the season. I knew I hadn't played well and I knew I was capable of playing better."

Three years of frustration had left their mark on Starr. Despite encouragement from his wife and his parents, he was depressed and doubtful about his future in football.

22

The hand off is as difficult as the pass. Here Starr demonstrates perfect technique in getting ball to his running back.

"I wasn't emotionally mature," he says. "Maybe I was too young to take so much disappointment. I should have been over the college letdown, but I still let it bother me. I didn't really have faith in myself, and that's one thing you can't hide in a family as close as a pro football club. I couldn't inspire confidence in the players, I couldn't be a leader, and leadership is probably the one most important quality a quarterback has to have."

The next season was no help. The Packers changed coaches, looking for a winner; instead, they had the worst season in the team's history, losing ten games, winning one, and tying one.

Starr played less than he had the year before and certainly the bad record was not his fault, but his confidence in himself was even more shaken.

"Confidence is the result of success," Starr says. "There aren't any confident losers. For four years, I hadn't succeeded in anything in football. When I went into a game, I acted confident, but that was only on the surface. Inside I was expecting to fail, and so I did."

Still, Bart did not consider quitting. All during the bad years, he continued to work hard to improve himself, working hard in practice, trying to improve his knowledge of the game and his technique, and he was, surely, growing better and better, even though he did not realize it himself.

"The Lord was good enough to give me perseverance," he says. "I needed it. I worked and worked and eventually it paid off. I don't think I was really a natural quarterback. What I achieved, I had to do by application and concentration. I found out that anyone who is really determined to do something he wants to do will make progress if he keeps plugging away. It worked that way for me, anyway."

Actually, at this point in his career, Bart needed only a final push to lift him from the ranks of journeymen quarterbacks to superstar. In 1959, he got that push.

The big change in his luck, and indeed in his life, came when Vincent Lombardi came to Green Bay in 1959 as the new head coach. Lombardi had been an assistant coach for the New York Giants and, before that, an assistant to Colonel Earl Blaik, the head coach at West Point. He knew football as well as any man but, more importantly, he had a vibrant, powerful personality that could animate a team and a strong sense of discipline, learned at the military academy.

He was a short, stocky, very positive man, with a wide smile and an iron will. He had been used to winning all his life and he inspired the Packers with a belief in their ability to win.

Lombardi did not promise the Packers an easy road to success. He told them that he would make them champions, but that they would have to pay the price of hard, hard work, loyalty, and faith in him and themselves.

He was not impressed by Starr.

"I looked at the movies of the club and decided that the first thing I needed to win was help at quarterback," he said later. "I didn't think Starr or Parilli could do the job, so I traded for Lamar McHan."

"That was a real shock," Starr says. "I wasn't happy at all when Mr. Lombardi traded for another quarterback. I had been in the league for three years and it looked like I might be the number-two quarterback for the rest of my life. But I never even considered quitting. It was another challenge."

Lombardi called his quarterbacks in early, so that he could give them the new offenses he had in mind. His play book—the thick loose-leaf book of all the plays that make up an offense—differed considerably from the offense Starr had learned, but he was not worried about learning it.

"I was impressed with Lombardi the first time I met him, even if he wasn't that impressed with me," Starr says. "I didn't blame him for bringing in a new quarterback, but I decided to show him I could do the job. All you had to do was talk to him to get the feeling he generated of confidence and ability and determination. He was a well-organized, disciplined man and an inspirational man, too."

After a three-week cram course in Lombardi-style football, Starr was ready when the rest of the club reported to training camp. He had learned the play book cold, so that he was never in doubt when he called plays in practice or in the course of a game.

Nevertheless, Lombardi began the season with McHan as the number-one quarterback and kept him there until the season was nearly half over.

It wasn't until Thanksgiving Day, when Green Bay played the Detroit Lions in Detroit, that Bart was given the opportunity to be a starter. He played well and the Packers won, and Bart started nearly all of the remaining games. But he was still unsure of himself and doubtful of his ability to hold the starting job.

That changed for good in the last game of that season, against the San Francisco 49ers in San Francisco. It is not often that one game can make a great quarterback out of only a good one, but in this case it happened, almost miraculously.

"I had studied Lombardi's offense and his ideas about attacking the different defenses," Starr says. "A lot of the success depends on the ability of the quarterback to read keys, the things a defensive player does to indicate what kind of defense they are playing. Defenses are complicated, and they change from play to play, from man to man to zone to combination zone and man to man, and if you don't recognize them immediately, you get into trouble."

"I knew all the theory," he goes on. "I mean I knew what keys to look for and I had spent a lot of time watching movies of the other teams' defenses, but in the middle of a game, when you're dropping back to set up to throw the ball, it looks different, not as clear.

"But on that afternoon in San Francisco, all at once, everything fell into place. It was like someone had taken a veil from in front of my face. I *knew* the keys."

The faculty that had come to him so suddenly in the San Francisco game has stayed with him ever since, and it was partly responsible for the sudden improvement of the Packers the following year. Then the club won the championship of the Western Division of

In 1966 league game against Browns, Starr is all alone as he releases pass.

the National Football League. The players were becoming a great football team, but not only because of the improvement in Starr.

Paul Hornung and Jim Taylor were the running backs, both of them good enough to be all-pros. Starr had exceptionally fine pass receivers to throw to in Boyd Dowler and Max McGee and a defense that was beginning to jell into one of the finest units in the history of the game.

Starr shared the quarterbacking with McHan for a little while, but by mid-season he was solidly installed as the starter. At the end of the year, he closed out the season by leading the club to three victories in a row.

Then Green Bay played the Philadelphia Eagles for the NFL championship. Quarterback for the Eagles was Norman Van Brocklin, a ten-year veteran who had once led the Los Angeles Rams to a championship and who was one of the wiliest quarterbacks in the business.

Actually, the Packers probably had better personnel than the Eagles, but Starr, even after the most satisfactory year he had had in a long time, could not match the battle-tested skill and experience of Van Brocklin. On a wet, slippery field in Philadelphia, the Packers lost, 17–13.

Chuck Bednarik, a grizzled veteran who had played center and linebacker for the Eagles for fifteen years, said after the game, "The difference was that we had the big gun at quarterback and they didn't."

If Starr wasn't a big gun that year, he was to be from then on. He had shown enough ability so that in the off season Lombardi traded Lamar McHan to the Baltimore Colts for a draft choice.

"If you want to win, you have to go with one quarterback who runs the club," he said when he made the deal. "Bart proved he was our number one during the last half of last season, and he'll be my number one next season."

Starr proved Lombardi's theory in 1961. He started every one of the fourteen league games, and the Packers won the division title again, with eleven victories and only three losses.

Early in that year, in a game against the rough, physical Chicago Bears, he cleared another hurdle on his way to greatness. He was a quiet man, mild-mannered and a trifle diffident off the field, and some of the Packers still had not recognized him as a leader because he did not fit the stereotype of the tough, mean pro football player. Even when he was battered by the big defensive players, he got up without complaint and without reacting to what had happened to him.

"A lot of guys still thought he was a pussycat, even though he was winning games," one old Packer said. "But in the Bear game he was getting a hard time from one of their defensive ends, and when the guy said something to him after he had flattened Bart for about the fourth time, Bart came up swinging. We bought him after that."

By now he was the complete quarterback, with the physical skills, the confidence, the aggressiveness, and the know-how to take a team to a championship. That is what he did in 1961.

30

Running Back Paul Hornung explains play he thinks will work while Fullback Jim Taylor (center) and Starr listen.

He demonstrated just how much he had learned and how much he had matured in the fifth game of the season, against the strong Cleveland Browns before 75,049 people in Cleveland's Municipal Stadium. It was a big game for Green Bay because, coming off their first loss of the season to Detroit, they were facing one of the really powerful clubs in pro football.

No one could have been better than Starr was that day, under strong pressure to win. He threw nineteen passes and completed seventeen. One of the incomplete passes came when Paul Hornung dropped a short toss, and the other Starr threw away purposely when his intended receivers were not open.

This time the Packers played the New York Giants for the league championship and had the advantage of playing the championship game in their own stadium. It was, as usual in Green Bay in December, a bitterly cold day, but the Packers were accustomed to cold weather.

Again Bart had a spectacular day. Throwing through a blustery, brisk wind in the cold, he completed ten of nineteen passes, and three of the completions were for touchdowns. Only Paul Hornung, the Golden Boy from Notre Dame, contributed more to the Packer victory; he scored three touchdowns and kicked three field goals and was chosen the outstanding player of the game as the Packers won, 37–0.

The year and the impressive day he had had against the Giants meant that, finally, Starr had arrived.

"Starr might have been the outstanding player in

that championship game if he had thrown the ball more," one of the Packer assistant coaches said later. "We knew we could throw on the Giants all afternoon. But the running game was going and we had control of the game and Bart didn't want to take any chances. He never thinks of personal glory. He let Paul get that because he's a team man and a leader and I doubt that he ever thought of his own statistics, other than the touchdowns he put on the board. That's why he's a real leader now. The players know how he feels."

Chapter 3

The Packers, with Starr playing brilliantly, won ten games in a row in 1962 before they went to Detroit for their traditional Thanksgiving game with the Lions. The game, of course, was played on Thursday, which poses a difficult problem for the visiting team. They have only Monday, Tuesday, and Wednesday to prepare and must travel to Detroit on Wednesday, as well.

The Lions drubbed the Packers, 26–14, and they gave Starr what was probably the worst afternoon of his life as a football player. They blitzed on nearly every play, with the linebackers coming in on him with the defensive linemen, and time and again he was dumped behind the line of scrimmage before he could get his pass away.

He took a brutal physical beating in the first half, but he took it without complaint, and in the second half he threw for two touchdowns in the teeth of the rush.

"You have days like that," he said after the game. "It wasn't anyone's fault. Give the Lions credit. They

This is what happens when pass blocking breaks down.
Starr is buried by a Viking lineman.

had a great pass rush, they wanted to win more than we did. I think we'll bounce back."

That was the only game the Packers lost that year. Their next game was against the Los Angeles Rams in Milwaukee, and they destroyed the Rams, 41–10. For the second year in a row, they won the Western Conference Championship, and they played the Giants again, this time in Yankee Stadium.

The day was cold and the wind blew, but the weather did not bother the Giants much in their home stadium. Starr, throwing through the swirling winds, with hands numb from cold, had a difficult time completing passes. Each stadium in the NFL has different characteristics for passers; the winds are not constant and the ball is carried in a different direction when the quarterback lets it go.

Starr completed only ten of twenty-two passes, but he never threw an interception and he selected running plays wisely for Jim Taylor and Paul Hornung. Green Bay won its second NFL championship in a row, 16–7, when Jerry Kramer iced the game by kicking a forty-nine-yard field goal through lowering weather and howling winds.

After their second straight world championship, the Packers were beginning to get recognition as one of the best teams in pro football history. But most pro football critics did not attribute that excellence to Starr; John Unitas was playing for the Baltimore Colts and Unitas had become a legend in his own time. He was a more spectacular, daring quarterback than Starr, but not a better one. Bart avoided arguments about whether he was a better quarterback than Unitas, but, over the years, he won more championships than Unitas.

"John is a great quarterback," he said. "I consider it an honor to be compared with him."

"We're not the same kind of people," Unitas said. "Bart is a fine quarterback, but he calls plays to control the ball and I gamble. I throw anytime. He throws when the odds are in his favor. But he's a heck of a passer. Look at his statistics. On the scoreboard."

Almost everyone expected the Packers to win the championship again in 1963, since they had back almost exactly the same team that had won it the year before. Indeed, they should have. They lost only two games, but both of them were to the Chicago Bears, and the Bears won the division championship and beat the Y. A. Tittle-led New York Giants for the championship in Chicago, 14–10. Bart, after breaking his hand in the sixth game of the season against the St. Louis Cardinals, missed four games. The Packers, with Zeke Bratkowski at quarterback, won three of them, but they lost the crucial fourth game against the Bears, 26–7.

"I didn't like losing," Bart said after the season. "No one does. But by then I had learned to accept defeat with grace if not with pleasure. You can't waste time going over old losses. You have to look ahead. I knew we had a good ball club and I knew we could win. So I didn't worry about one bad year."

A bad season and a bad game are not so different.

"I learned to forget about defeat the year before

Starr, after the injury, listens to scouts on press-box phone
while Zeke Bratkowski, helmet under his arm, prepares to
take over.

when Detroit racked us up on Thanksgiving Day," Bart said. "The Bears reminded me of Detroit. No matter what we tried to do, they were a play ahead of us. I remember once, in the Detroit game, I knew they were going to blitz—they did most of the time—and I tried to take advantage of them. They had been sending in their linebackers, so I figured I could hit Ron Kramer, our tight end, with a quick pass in the hole a linebacker leaves when he blitzes. Wayne Walker was their linebacker on that side and he moved up like he was going to rush, but when the ball was snapped, he dropped off into the pass pattern and I couldn't hit Ron."

He looked at a diagram of the play in the Green Bay dressing room and shook his head.

"It should have worked," he said. "But some days nothing works. For two days in 1963, not enough worked against the Bears. They won and we lost and they deserved the championship."

The Packers beat the Bears in the first game of the 1964 season, but in the second game Starr made a mistake that may have cost the club the championship that year. He had gained enough confidence in himself to admit the mistake and not let himself be destroyed by it.

Green Bay played a strong Baltimore team in that second game and, late in the second half, they trailed by a point, 21–20. They had the ball and Starr called time out so that he could confer with coach Lombardi on the sideline. Lombardi advised him to throw to Kramer, the big, powerful tight end.

In the huddle, Bart called the play Lombardi had suggested, but he did not see Kramer, the intended receiver, when he dropped back to pass and therefore tried to hit Max McGee, a wide receiver. A Baltimore defensive back dropped off and intercepted the pass, and after the game Lombardi raised Cain with Starr in the dressing room. Starr knew he had made a mistake, so he did not argue, but when he got home that night, he cried in frustration.

But he learned, even from mistakes.

"After I got over kicking myself for blowing the play," he said later, "I forgot about it. Before that, when I made a mistake, I couldn't stop thinking about it. But I forgot about this one and so did Lombardi and the rest of the team. You can't go back and correct yesterday's mistakes."

The Packers finished second that year and lost to the Cardinals in Miami in the second-place bowl. Lombardi did not like to lose. When they began practice in 1965, he remembered two years of second-place finishes, and the club suffered for it.

"You're better than a second-place team," he said when they got to training camp. "You quit paying the price. This year, you pay the price."

"He nearly killed us," Starr said later. "He always worked us hard, but he worked us until we dropped. But we knew we had it coming."

All the hard work nearly went for nothing. Jerry Kramer, the all-pro guard, had been sick during the off season and could not play; then Fuzzy Thurston, another great veteran guard, hurt his leg, so that the

During 1965 championship game against Cleveland, Starr confers with head coach Vince Lombardi.

Packers lacked blocking strength in the offensive line early in the season.

With a weakened offensive line, the Packers did not move the ball as easily as they had in previous years. The blocking was not so well coordinated and sharp as it had been and Starr didn't have time to throw and there were no holes for the backs to run through.

But the defense picked up the slack, and even though Starr was not putting points on the board, the Packers managed to win. So did the Baltimore Colts, with Johnny Unitas engineering a strong offense. By the time the Packers met the Colts in Baltimore in the next to the last season game of the year, the Packers were a half game behind the Colts and had to beat them.

They came into Baltimore on a Tuesday, three days before they would normally have arrived for an away game. Kramer and Thurston were healthy and the club was playing at its peak. Lombardi didn't give them a pep talk before they took the field.

"He wasn't much for pep talks," Starr remembers. "Once in a while he would say a few words and you felt them. This time he said, 'I don't think I have to tell you how much this game means. But I would like to say one thing. Whether you win, lose, or draw, the way you have played this season has made me proud to be your coach.' "

They made him proud again on a cold, foggy afternoon as Hornung scored five touchdowns and Starr directed the team flawlessly, completing ten of nineteen passes, one for a touchdown.

Starr leaves the field with an injury after first play against the Colts in 1965 play-off game.

Starr, with good protection, throws a pass completed against Cleveland.

The club had a letdown the next week, against San Francisco in the Bay City, and settled for a tie, which left them in a tie with Baltimore for the conference title. The play-off was in Green Bay.

Playing behind Starr was Zeke Bratkowski, who was a year older than Bart and who had played with the Los Angeles Rams and the Chicago Bears before he joined the Packers as the number-two quarterback. He and Starr were close friends, probably because Bart, who had occupied the same number-two position for a long time, could sympathize with Zeke.

Before the play-off game, Bart said, "Most people don't realize how much a good number-two quarterback can help. He's on the phones, for one thing, relaying plays down from the coaches in the press box. And with a man who has had his experience in tough games, he can tell you a lot on the sideline. And finally, you know if anything happens to you, there's a competent man waiting on the sidelines to take over."

Bart was hurt on the first play of the play-off with Baltimore, and Zeke came in and won the game in overtime.

Starr, who could barely raise his arm to throw, was not the only injured Packer after the Baltimore play-off game. Jim Taylor, the premier running fullback, had a sore leg, and Paul Hornung, the Golden Boy, had a twisted knee, sore ribs, and a sprained wrist.

"We're not very healthy," Lombardi said before the championship game with Cleveland, but he was smiling. "These men are pros and they will play. They can play with pain or bad luck."

The power of the Cleveland team was Jim Brown, who may have been the finest running back of all time. He was a giant of a runner, with exceptional speed, fluid moves, and extraordinary acceleration, and during his long career he led the NFL in ground-gaining almost every year. Taylor, of Green Bay, was usually a reluctant second.

The two teams had scouted each other well, studying movies of previous games and deciding what the tendencies were in any situation, on offense or defense. Green Bay knew that when Brown lined up behind the quarterback with the other running back to his right, he would take the ball and run to his right. They overshifted their defense, and Brown did not run far in this game.

The Browns knew that when Taylor or Hornung lined up behind the quarterback with a running back to the right, they went the other way. In spite of that, the Packer running game worked well enough to give them a 10–0 lead at the half as the Green Bay offensive line handled the Brown defenders.

The Browns rallied to within a point at 13–12 in the third period, and when the Packers took over on the Cleveland thirty-five-yard line, first and ten, Starr knew he had to change the attacking pattern. The Browns were used to Hornung or Taylor running to their left out of the set with one or the other of them directly behind the quarterback, and they had adjusted their defenses to stop that.

"During the first half I wanted them to think I always called that kind of running play," Bart said after

46

the game. "We wanted to make them go in motion that way before the play got started, and when I called a counter, they did. We had made them develop a bad habit, and when we took advantage of it, it worked."

He called a play with a fake to Taylor to the left and a hand-off to Hornung to the right, and Paul went twenty yards down to the Cleveland fifteen-yard line.

Two plays later, Hornung scored and Green Bay won the game and the championship, 23–12.

"This is the best win we have ever had," Lombardi said after the game. "It came so hard, all year long. People hurt, the offense out of kilter. Nothing went right. But they never quit. Everything was hard, but they never quit. The season and the play-off. Everything. When you win this way, you earned it."

"It was a hard season," Starr said thoughtfully, his face, as always, serious. "But it was a good one. It was a test, a challenge. When you sacrifice, you appreciate what you have won. We sacrificed."

Chapter

The next year, 1966, the Packers proved their claim to be the best team in football and Bart went a long way toward making good the claims other people had made about his being the best quarterback.

This was the first year that the American Football League and the National Football League met in a post-season play-off to determine the world championship of professional football.

The National Football League had been in existence for forty-five years, the AFL for seven. Obviously, the NFL had the veteran players. Now, for the first time, the champions of the two leagues would meet in a post-season game to determine which was indeed the better.

The Packers were now reaching the peak of their power. Bart was a blooded, intelligent, strong quarterback; for two of the last three years he had led the NFL in passing and the Packers lost only two games in winning their second straight championship of the league. He put the ball in the air 251 times, completed

156 passes, and had only 3 interceptions, one of the best records any pro quarterback has ever compiled.

The last game of the season said something about the Packers and their extraordinary desire to win. They had already clinched their division championship and they were playing the Los Angeles Rams, a club that had to win the game to get into the play-offs.

"It would have been easy for us to let down in this game," Bart said after it was over. "I was hurt and I did not play at all, but that didn't make that much difference because Zeke was such a good quarterback. But we had already wrapped up the conference title and some people thought that coach Lombardi would rest some of his better players to get them ready for the big game against Dallas in the play-off. And they figured that none of the players would really be excited about a game that really meant almost nothing to us."

Lombardi did not believe in his team, his players, individually, or himself giving anything less than the best. Before the game, he talked to the team.

"If you go out there and don't do your best," he told them, "you're cheating yourself. You'll be cheating the rest of the team, too, and all the people in Green Bay who believe in you. The Lord gave you the ability to be as good as you are, and if you don't use all the ability He gave you, you're cheating your Maker, too."

The Packers didn't cheat anyone. They won the game.

So they played the Dallas Cowboys for the National Football League championship, with the Super Bowl awaiting the winner of that game.

49

Dallas Cowboys are deep in Green Bay territory in 1966 championship game and (left to right), coach Red Cochrane, Starr, Hornung, Bratkowski, and Coach Lombardi reflect concern.

The Cowboys were a fine football team and the game was played in the Cotton Bowl in Dallas, before 75,000 Dallas fans.

But the Packers had a significant advantage. They had been there before. Pressure games were nothing new either to the club or to Starr. They had, as usual, scouted the Cowboys thoroughly, and Starr knew their weaknesses on defense so well that he did not have to think about them.

"We had a special play to open the game," Bart said when it was over and he was back in the dressing room. "The Cowboys had great pursuit on defense and we took advantage of it."

Pursuit cuts down on long gainers since all of the players on the defense go for the ballcarrier, cutting off his routes to open ground. But if all the defenders go after the obvious ballcarrier, a counter, against the flow of the play, can work.

"We put the counter in to defeat the pursuit," Starr explained. "I faked a handoff to Jim Taylor going one way, and when the Cowboy defense reacted to his movement, I handed the ball to Elijah Pitts, cutting back in the other direction, against the grain of the pursuit. The first play gained thirty-two yards and we were on our way."

They were on their way with a vengeance not long after; Pitts caught a seventeen-yard pass from Starr for a Green Bay touchdown, Dallas fumbled a kickoff and had the ball run in for another touchdown, and the young Cowboys were behind 14–0 before they had had possession of the ball.

But, as so often happens when touchdowns come too easily, the Packers let down.

"We relaxed and they didn't give up," Starr said later. "I made it a point to tell Don Meredith [the Dallas quarterback] how much I admired the way they came back."

The undaunted Cowboys scored two touchdowns and a field goal, and the uninspired Packers could manage only a field goal during the rest of the first half, so that when the second period ended, the Green Bay margin had been reduced to 21–17. Dallas scored on a meticulous thirteen-play drive engineered by Meredith and a brilliant twenty-three-yard run by their fine fullback, Don Perkins. The Dallas defense had shut down on the Green Bay running and Bart was forced to put the ball in the air more often.

His passing, as usual, was effective. With the game in its waning moments, he had completed three touchdown passes, to Carroll Dale, Max McGee, and Boyd Dowler, and the Packers were again comfortably ahead, 34–20.

But Meredith and his teammates did not give up. Don took advantage of a Green Bay misfortune when one of the Packer defensive backs fell, leaving receiver Frank Clarke wide open for a pass that covered sixty-six yards and resulted in a touchdown that brought the Cowboys to within a touchdown of Green Bay.

The Cowboy defenders stopped the Packers again, and again the Dallas offense moved the ball so that, with only a minute and a half to play, the Cowboys were in possession of the ball on the Green Bay two-yard line.

And this is what happens when the quarterback is buried. Starr, on the line, has just been intercepted.

Starr, of course, was watching helplessly from the sideline at this point, since the defensive team was on the field.

"I can't explain why," he said after the game, "but I wasn't worried. I knew our defense would come up with a big play and stop Dallas. They had made the big plays all year, and I knew they would this time, too."

Tom Brown, the defensive back who had fallen to free Clarke for the Dallas touchdown, redeemed himself by making the big play, with help from Dave Robinson, a big, very mobile linebacker. It came on fourth down, when Meredith rolled out to his right, intending either to run or to throw to a free receiver if he could find one. It was a good, intelligent call.

"I thought a roll out would give me two chances to score," Don Meredith said after the game. "If all of my receivers were covered, I could run. I faked a hand off to a back running into the line because I thought that would freeze Robinson so that he couldn't cut me off to the outside. But he didn't buy the fake."

Actually, Robinson did take the fake for a split second. By the time he reacted to the threat of the run, the guard who would have blocked him had gone by him and he cut behind the guard and hit Meredith just as he started to throw the ball. The ball wobbled weakly into the end zone and Brown, who had covered the intended receiver, intercepted it to save the Packer victory, 34–27.

Normally this game for the NFL championship would have spelled the end of the season, but the NFL and the AFL had agreed to peace terms and to a game

54

between their respective league champions, so the Packers went on to play in the first Super Bowl, on January 15, 1967, against the Kansas City Chiefs, champions of the AFL.

It was an even bigger game than the one with Dallas, because for years the fans and players of the AFL had maintained that they were as good as or better than the older NFL teams. The arguments between the fans and players of the two leagues were long and bitter; this game would settle those arguments, and the players on both teams involved felt the enormous pressure long before the game was played.

For the Packers, the game presented special problems, especially for Starr, the quarterback.

They trained at Santa Barbara, a seacoast town about 120 miles north of Los Angeles, where the game would be played. When they reported for practice a week before the game, Lombardi told them that they were not only being given the chance to be the first Super Bowl champions in football history, but they were representing, for the first time, more than Green Bay. They were the representatives of the National Football League.

"I wasn't an offensive guard for Green Bay," said Fuzzy Thurston, after the game. "I knew that when I was blocking on Buck Buchanan [the Kansas City defensive tackle] in the Coliseum in Super Bowl, I wasn't just old Fuzz from Green Bay. I was every guard in the NFL blocking on every tackle in the AFL. If I had blown it, I would have blown it for the league, not just me or the Packers."

Starr getting off pass just in time against Kansas City in first Super Bowl game, won by Green Bay.

Starr and the rest of the team felt the same way.

"We knew they were a good ball club," Bart said. "Shucks, you don't win a league championship unless you're a fine team. But we were proud of what we had done and we knew that all the things we had accomplished would have been ruined if we had lost to them. No one would remember that we had won the National Football League championship. If we had lost to Kansas City, the one thing everyone would remember was that the Green Bay team of 1966 was the team which lost the first Super Bowl game ever played."

The Kansas City Chiefs, of course, were as proud as the Packers; unfortunately for them, they were not as good.

The game, for both teams, was different and difficult simply because they had never played each other before and were unfamiliar with each other's offense and defense. Even the study of game films of previous games did not help Bart much, because he did not know the players against whom the Chiefs were operating.

"I know, when I'm watching one of the NFL teams in action against another, how good the individuals are because I have played against them," he said before the game. "But watching the Chiefs playing against other teams in the AFL was like watching strangers. I didn't know how fast the defensive backs were and I couldn't read their defenses very well. So I had to be very careful for a while, until I could figure them out."

He had decided, from watching the movies of the Chiefs, that he would be able to throw passes to his receivers in the area covered by the Kansas City corner-backs, but he tested that theory with fake patterns before he tried it.

When he thought the time was ripe, he called a pass to McGee, who was being covered, man to man, by Willie Mitchell, one of the best defensive backs in the AFL. McGee gave Mitchell a quick head and shoulder fake to the outside, then broke over the middle, and Starr's pass found him wide open for a thirty-seven-yard touchdown.

"They played a tough man to man," Starr said. "But once we found out that our wide receivers could beat them man to man, they were dead."

The Packer defense had the same problems and played as cautiously as the offense early in the game. They were not quite sure how good—or bad—the Chief attack was, and they concentrated on not making mistakes. Some of their normal defenses were useless against the Chiefs; while they were adjusting to the new look, they gave up a touchdown that tied the game at 7–7.

But by the time the Chiefs had scored the tying touchdown, Starr and the Packer offensive team had worked out the answers to the Chief defense. Bart did not have to be overly cautious anymore; he could use all the weapons in his well-stocked arsenal, and in the second quarter he began to do just that. He had discovered that the Packers could run when they had to and that, indeed, his wide receivers could beat the Chief cornerbacks to either the inside or the outside.

Using his tools as aptly as a great surgeon, he

*Jim Taylor drives through Kansas City line for touchdown
as Starr (15) looks on.*

marched the Green Bay team seventy-three yards in thirteen plays to put them ahead 14–7. On the drive, he had a long touchdown pass called back for a penalty; the play, aside from the penalty, was a perfect example of how clearly Starr had analyzed the weakness of the Chief defenses.

The play took advantage, really, of a strength of one of the Chief cornerbacks. His name was Fred Williamson, but his nickname was "the Hammer" because of the impact he generated in making tackles. He played close to the line, anxious to move up to make a tackle against the run.

So Starr called a play that looked like a run to the Hammer's side and the Hammer, reading run, came up to the line of scrimmage very quickly.

Carroll Dale, the Packer wide receiver he should have been covering, went by him just as quickly and caught the pass for a touchdown, but Green Bay had been off side and the play was called back.

So Starr took the touchdown in short bites instead of a big gulp, throwing to his wide receivers for short gains until the club reached the Kansas City fourteen-yard line. Then he called a power sweep, with the guards pulling ahead of Taylor, who scored behind a wall of blockers. The half ended with Green Bay ahead, 14–10.

To the AFL fans, the game had seemed to be even; what they did not realize was that the Packers had finished testing the Chief defense and offense and were ready to apply what they had learned, in the second half.

Starr had experimented with the tools at his disposal in the first half; in the second half he took the most effective tools and destroyed Kansas City. The Green Bay defense had diagnosed the Kansas offense just as efficiently; they knew what Kansas City could do best and what they had to do to keep them from doing it.

"We were a little careful in the first half," said Willie Davis, an all-pro end and the captain of the Packer defense. "In the second half, we knew what to do and we let it all out. We went after them."

The defense started by intercepting a Chief pass just after the second half began. Davis put pressure on Len Dawson, the Kansas quarterback, and when he hurried his pass, Willie Wood, the Packer strong safety, intercepted the ball and returned it to the Chief five-yard line.

Starr called a power sweep, the Packers scored, and the game, practically, was over. Starr passed to McGee for thirteen yards and another touchdown, the Packer defense dominated the Chiefs, and when it was all over, Green Bay had won, 35–10. Appropriately, on one of the last plays of the game, the Hammer, who was so proud of his ability to hit hard, was knocked out. When he went down, Wood, on the sideline, laughed.

"Looks like the Hammer got nailed," he said.

"We played very well," Starr said later. "When everyone on the team plays as well as that, it's pretty easy to call the signals. The credit for winning the first Super Bowl goes to every player on the club and to coach Lombardi and his assistants."

Starr, of course, was being a bit too modest.

"Bart picks a weak spot and hits it better than any quarterback I ever saw," one of the Kansas City defensive backs said. "He really picked our pass defense to pieces. Every time they had third and long yardage, he made it. You can't beat that."

"He's a good quarterback," another Chief said. "He's every bit as good as the best quarterback in our league."

That was damning Starr with faint praise. He was better. He was chosen all-pro by the Associated Press, the United Press, and every other organization that picks all-pros. He was named the most valuable player in the Super Bowl and given the Jim Thorpe award, emblematic of the best player in pro football.

But he accepted the honors with the same attitude with which he had accepted previous disappointments. He had known that he was better than his failures; now he knew that he was not alone to get the credit for his success.

"The honors are good," he said after the season had ended. "Anyone who says he doesn't like being recognized is a liar. But the things I have done I owe to the guys who played with me and the men who coached us. You have an enormous advantage playing on a good team, and not just because the offensive players are good. To show you what I mean, just think of how lucky I am to practice against our defense. They're so good that Sunday seems easy by comparison. It's a relief to call plays against another club."

Chapter **5**

Unfortunately fame in pro football, as in most of life, lasts only for a season. During the off season after the Super Bowl triumph, Starr was feted on radio and TV, at lunches and dinners. He is a gentle, thoughtful man, and he was willing to stand for hours giving. autographs to children and talking to strangers, but he still found time to keep in condition by running every day. He does not smoke or drink; he worked especially hard on conditioning during that slack time because he knew that every club in the league would have its sights set on the Packers the next year.

"I remembered how it was when we were down," he said, wryly. "We saved the big game for the champion. So every other club was saving their big game for us, even during the exhibitions."

During the exhibitions in 1967, Bart picked up severely bruised ribs, which slowed down his training. When he recovered from the damaged ribs, he had his right thumb sprained in another exhibition game, a much more serious injury for a passer. With a sore and

A man's best friend is his dog and, in this case, Bart's wife, Cherry.

swollen thumb, he had difficulty grasping the ball properly for a pass or holding it securely for a hand-off to one of his running backs. And the Packers, who had had almost no injuries in 1966, made up for that in 1967.

Jim Taylor and Paul Hornung, the superb tandem of running backs, were gone, Hornung with an injured neck and Taylor by trade. Their replacements were good but inexperienced. Experience, as Starr knew very well, is the one most important quality in a pro football player.

The injury to Starr and the loss of the two great running backs made a much bigger difference than the average fan realizes.

Alex Karras, who was an all-pro defensive tackle for the Detroit Lions, once explained why.

"It doesn't take much to hurt even the best clubs," he said. "Just lose one or two real quality players. Green Bay had lost two, and Starr was hurt. They had a real problem. Their defense was about the same, but they couldn't run when they had to. You have to remember Taylor and Hornung weren't just great runners, they were great blockers, too. With the running shut off and Starr not able to pass as well as usual, they were in deep trouble. The defense can't do it all."

Karras qualified as an expert on the Packers. In the first league game of that year, he tackled Starr four times while he was attempting to pass. Throwing inaccurately because of the sore thumb, Bart had four passes intercepted, one more interception than he had thrown in the whole previous season.

The defense, however, did most of it the next week, when the Packers defeated the Chicago Bears, 13–10, despite the five interceptions Bart threw, his thumb still sore and his control of his passes uncertain. He was hurt again in that game and was unable to play against the Atlanta Falcons. He returned to action against the New York Giants in Yankee Stadium, and the mere fact that he was back gave the team a lift.

"We're used to Bart," said Forrest Gregg, Green Bay's all-pro offensive tackle. "Zeke Bratkowski did a good job filling in, but he's not Bart. There's a delicate balance in any offense, and when one element is off just a little, it hurts the operation of the machine. We've been lucky because the defense has played so well, because the offense hasn't been doing the job. With Bart back and healthy, I think we will. We know we can move the ball."

Starr wasn't exactly healthy. His right thumb was still sore, his ribs were bruised, and he had a tender shoulder, but none of the injuries were serious by pro football standards.

"You have to ignore the pain," he said. "It hurts, but if you think about the hurting, you can't think about playing."

At this point in the season, the Packers were 3–1–1. Another loss could very well put them out of contention for the championship, so the game was a big one. With the offense sputtering, the club had not looked as powerful as most experts had expected them to be; a loss to the Giants could very easily send them on a skid that would be fatal to their hopes.

The playing days are over. Starr is a coach now and can
spend more time with his family—Bret, in Bart's lap,
Bart, Jr., and Bart's wife, Cherry.

Starr hands off for key running play in division-playoff victory over the Los Angeles Rams in 1967.

The Packers started slowly and trailed the Giants, 14–10, at the half. Bart ached in all the places he had been hurt, but in the second half he rallied the team to a 48–21 victory.

"Starr was the difference," Lombardi said after the game. "He's a long way from a hundred percent, but he gave us a lift. We were down and he picked us up. We ran harder, blocked better, and won."

Starr had had to leave the game in the fourth period, and he was not as efficient as usual.

"He's still hurt," Lombardi went on. "He had deep receivers open twice and couldn't reach them. But we needed his ability as a leader and a tactician."

The players welcomed him back, too.

"No one was down on Starr in the early games when he was playing with pain," said Ray Nitschke, the Packer middle linebacker who was used to playing with pain himself. "You got to go with a guy like that. He's got pride and he helped us feel pride in ourselves. Sure, the defense had to work a lot harder, but we knew when Bart came around and Grabowski and Anderson got a little more experience, the offense would score."

Grabowski and Anderson were the young running backs who had replaced Taylor and Hornung.

The victory over the Giants was no magic answer to the Packer problems; for the rest of the season, the defense still carried the brunt most of the time, but the offense, with Starr getting better game by game, started carrying more and more of the load, and the Packers won their division championship.

They played the Los Angeles Rams for the Western Conference title; the Rams were young, big, and talented. They had won eleven games, lost one, and tied two over the season while the Packers had won nine, lost four, and tied one. Going into the play-off game in Milwaukee, the Rams were strong favorites, despite the bitterly cold weather.

During the season the Rams had defeated Green Bay 27–24, with Starr playing at only a fraction of his potential; for this game, finally, he was strong, with all of his injuries healed. The Packers won, easily.

"We played conservative ball in the first game," he said before this one. "A lot of that was because I just couldn't physically handle our whole offense. But this time we'll go for broke. If we lose this one, that's it. The season is over."

One of the toughest problems Starr faced was negating Deacon Jones, the very big, exceptionally fast defensive end for the Rams, who had hounded him unmercifully in the first game.

"We had to do something to slow the Deacon down," Starr said. "If you let him alone, he'll eat you alive. He'll come in like a freight train and you don't have time to get the ball away. So early in the play-off game, we ran right at him. We'd put two blockers on him and ride him out and run over his position until he had to begin to worry about stopping the run first and rushing the passer after that. Once you make a lineman play run first, pass second, you take away most of his rush."

The strategy worked; Jones's pass rush was blunted

70

and, with time to throw, Bart picked apart the Ram defense on the way to a 28–7 victory for the Packers.

Then came the sub-freezing game against the Dallas Cowboys, in which Starr carried the ball over for a touchdown in the closing seconds to win the NFL championship 21–17. The bitter cold may have inhibited the Cowboys a bit; they were used to playing in warmer weather.

"We had a hunch they were fair-weather players," Ray Nitschke said. "You don't get fair weather in Green Bay in January."

It was a long way from fair for the game. Fans who bought coffee in a faint hope of warming themselves found the coffee frozen before they could drink it, and the wife of the Dallas coach, closing her eyes against the penetrating wind, found them frozen shut before she could open them and had to hold her mittened hands over them before she could watch the game again.

Aside from the game-winning quarterback sneak, Starr called several other plays that demonstrated his ability to read defenses and remain cool—frigid, in this case—under pressure.

With third and a yard to go in the second quarter, he called the play that had nearly scored on Kansas City in the Super Bowl the year before, then only to be called back by a penalty. The Packers were on the Cowboy forty-three-yard line and the whole Dallas defense was drawn in close to the line to stop Ben Wilson, the fullback. Starr faked to Wilson, dropped back, and hit Boyd Dowler, throwing into the wind, for the touchdown.

But, as they had done the year before in Dallas, the Cowboys came back. Their fine defensive line began to penetrate, and eight times they sacked Starr before he could throw.

"It wasn't the offensive line breaking down," Bart said. "They did all they had to do. But the receivers couldn't make their cuts on the icy field and I couldn't find them. I held the ball too long."

If Starr was in trouble, so was Meredith, the Cowboy quarterback.

"My hands got colder every time I went on the field," he said. "When your hands are as cold as mine were, you can't wing the ball. When the wind is blowing as hard as it was, you *have* to wing the ball. If you can't put spin on it, it won't bore into the wind."

Meredith cut a hole in the front of his jersey during the half, so that he could tuck his hand into it between plays to keep it warm. His passing improved, and a special play, put in for this game, caught the Packers off guard.

Meredith handed off to Dan Reeves, a running back who had been a quarterback in college, and Reeves swung wide to his left, stopped, and threw a touchdown pass to Lance Rentzel to put the Cowboys ahead, 17–14.

"I was slow in reacting to the play," said Bob Jeter, the Packer defensive back at fault. "We knew Reeves could throw. He had thrown before. But we forgot and I took a step up against the run, then saw him cock his arm, and I said to myself, 'Lord, what have I done?' I tried to get back to cover Rentzel, but when I saw the ball in the air, I knew I was dead."

*The young fans do not forget and Starr always has time
for them.*

Eventually, of course, Starr won the game with the quarterback sneak. On the way to that last long yard, he again demonstrated his ability to pick apart a defense. He used some of the strengths of the Dallas defense to defeat it.

The Cowboy rush was quick and hard, so he threw short passes to his backs. The short passes worked well enough to carry down to the Cowboy eleven-yard line, where Bart came up with a brilliant call.

Bob Lilly, one of the Cowboy defensive tackles, is an all-time all-pro football player, regarded by many experts as the best tackle ever to play the game. He had shut off everything in his area all afternoon; the last place that the Cowboys expected the Packers to attack was his position.

"Lilly's fast as some backs," Bart explained later. "When Gale Gillingham [the guard blocking on Lilly] pulled to lead a sweep, Lilly would barrel through the hole he left and run the ballcarrier down from behind. So we decided to fool him."

Bart faked a hand-off to Anderson, swinging to his right, Gillingham pulled as if to lead the play, and Lilly went through the hole in pursuit of Anderson. Then Starr handed the ball to Chuck Mercein, another fullback, and Mercein cut back through the position Lilly had left vacant and reached the Dallas three-yard line. From that position, two plays later, Starr scored on the sneak.

Chapter

The victory over Dallas put the Packers into the Super Bowl again, on Jan. 14, 1968, this time against the Oakland Raiders in Miami's Super Bowl. The Raiders, in winning the American Football League championship, had won thirteen games and lost only one, a much more impressive record than Green Bay's 9–4–1.

Since the competition in the AFL was not as strong as that in the NFL, the Packers were strong favorites to win, despite the fact that some of them still had frostbitten fingers and toes as a result of the sub-freezing weather in Green Bay. The weather in Miami, as usual, was balmy.

Strangely enough, this game was anticlimactic. The emotional game had been against Dallas, when the club won against all odds in the closing seconds; too, it had played and won the first Super Bowl the previous year against Kansas City.

"That was the historic game," Starr said before the club played Oakland. "We respect this Oakland team and we know they will give us trouble and we'll do our best. Under coach Lombardi, you don't do anything else. But there is not the same motivation."

The Packers were not as sharp against Oakland as they had been in other games during the season, but they won easily enough, 33–14, and again Starr was named the most valuable player in the game.

He threw a sixty-two-yard touchdown pass to Dowler, led drives down to the Oakland thirty-two- and thirteen-yard lines, both resulting in field goals, and set up one score with a beautifully timed and executed pass to McGee that carried from the Green Bay forty-yard to the Oakland twenty-five-yard line. The pass was a bit off target, but McGee made a spectacular catch, reaching behind him with one hand to pull the ball in.

"Max made a great play, not me," said Starr after the game. "Give him all the credit for that one."

"That's not quite right," McGee said. "I had the safety beat and he suddenly woke up and came over to cover me, and Bart read his move and threw the ball behind me, away from him. That's why I had to reach back for it. If he had led me, the ball would probably have been picked off."

Back home in Green Bay, where he spends the off-season, Starr caught up on being with his wife and his sons, Bart, Jr., and Brett. Bart, ten, was a rabid Green Bay fan; sometimes, at games with his mother, he had heard his father booed during that season. Most of the time, of course, he heard him cheered.

"I got a car for most valuable player after Super Bowl," Starr said later. "But the biggest kick I got out

In second Super Bowl, against Oakland in Miami, Starr hands off to Donny Anderson on way to an easy win over Oakland.

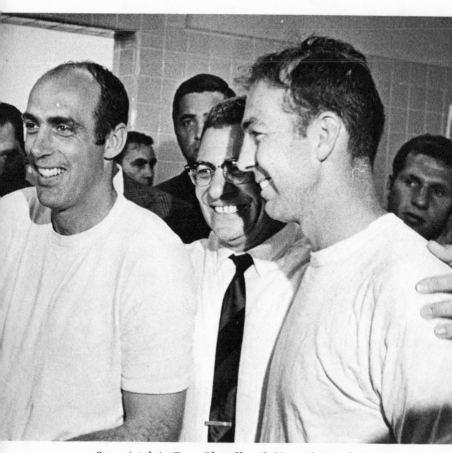

*Starr (right), Don Chandler (left), and Coach Lombardi
meet the press in the dressing room after victory over
Raiders in the second Super Bowl.*

of the season came after a bad game, not a big win."

Early on, when he had been hurt, Bart had a bad day against St. Louis, although Green Bay managed to win. He came back from the trip tired, bruised, and not very happy.

Starr had always rewarded his children when they did well; he would give Bart, Jr., a dime for a perfect grade in school, for instance.

When he finally climbed into bed that night, there was a note on his pillow from little Bart.

"Dear Dad," it said, "I thought you played a great game. Love, Bart."

Two dimes were Scotch-taped to the note.

Chapter 7

In the four years following that Super Bowl victory, the Packers—and Starr—suffered a series of misfortunes.

Coach Lombardi gave up coaching to become general manager and a year after that resigned to accept a job with the Washington Redskins. Two years later, he died suddenly.

In 1968, the year after the second Super Bowl championship, with Phil Bengtson coaching in place of Lombardi and Starr hurt much of the time, the team lost its division title to Baltimore. Starr was not able to play as much as he would have liked to, but he made no excuses.

"I've played hurt before," he said when the season was over. "We had a lot of other injuries, too. It wasn't anyone's fault, certainly not Phil Bengtson's."

Starr had injured his shoulder, an injury that did not at first appear to be any more serious than others he had played with and recovered from. But for the next three years, the shoulder was to plague him.

Starr moves away from the strong rush of Minnesota all-pro Carl Eller (81) in game against Vikings.

At the end of the 1970 season, in which Green Bay won only six games and lost eight, Starr knew he had to have expert repair work on his passing arm. He had lost the zip that Rote had told him was necessary for a pro quarterback, and the shoulder hurt whenever he threw the ball.

He went into the Mayo Brothers Clinic in Minnesota for a thorough examination, which lasted several days. When he came back to Green Bay to meet the new Packer head coach, Dan Devine, he felt cheerful.

"The doctors tell me the arm is fine now," he told a friend. "It's still a little weaker than the other one and I had a torn biceps muscle part of the season, but there is no structural damage in the shoulder. All I have to do is take the exercises they have given me to do, and it will get stronger."

Unfortunately the shoulder was hurt again in 1971, and Starr, for the first time in many years, was not the number-one quarterback for the Packers. Under Devine, they improved, but Bart was forced to sit on the sidelines and watch another young Alabama quarterback, Scott Hunter, run the team. He tried to come back late in the season, but his shoulder was still weak and he did not throw well.

When the season ended, most experts felt that Starr was through as a player. His name was mentioned for several coaching jobs; there was no question but that he would make a fine coach when his playing days were over.

But Starr ignored the coaching offers and went back to the hard work and exercise that had paid off

The glory years are over. It is 1971 and the New Orleans Saints are putting tremendous pressure on Starr.

The road back is long and uphill. Here, in 1971, Bart runs the steps in the Packer Stadium trying to regain his strength.

for him years before, when he came up to the Packers.

But by the beginning of training camp in 1972, he realized that his arm was not strong enough to justify his playing and he retired as a player. Bart now coaches the young Packer quarterbacks.

"He's like an encyclopedia," says Hunter. "We learn something new from him every day."

He teaches them perseverance and courage as well as football, and he does it by example.

Starr, injured and unable to throw, unhappily watches

his teammates prepare for a game in Miami.

After graduating from the University of Texas at Austin, Tex Maule became a sports writer for the Dallas *Morning News*. He left Dallas to be the Publicity Director for the Los Angeles Rams football team and later returned to be a sportswriter for the *Dallas News*.

Since 1957, Mr. Maule has been a Senior Editor at *Sports Illustrated*, specializing in the coverage of football. He is the author of many books, both fiction and non-fiction, on various aspects of football.

His coverage of sporting events for *Sports Illustrated* keeps Mr. Maule traveling a great deal of the time, but New York City is considered home.